Management of Educational Resources: 2 Effective Primary Schools

A report by
H M Inspectors of Schools

Scottish Education Department

HMSO

© Crown copyright 1989
First published 1989

ISBN 0 11 493517 3

Contents

Page

FOREWORD

INTRODUCTION

1. EFFECTIVE LEARNING AND TEACHING   1

2. ETHOS AND PARTNERSHIP   9

3. LEADERSHIP AND MANAGEMENT   16

4. ACCOUNTABILITY AND EVALUATION   26

Foreword

The importance of promoting good management and of achieving value for money in education was recognised in the establishment early in 1985 of the Management of Educational Resources Unit (MERU) within HM Inspectorate. The aim of the Unit is to increase management expertise and value for money within and beyond the Scottish Education Department. The work involves analysing and evaluating inspection and other evidence on the management of educational resources, contributing to the inspection of management in schools and colleges, producing working papers for use within the Department and elsewhere, developing performance indicators and undertaking costing exercises.

This report, the second in a series*, was written by a team drawn from MERU and other members of HM Inspectorate closely involved with the monitoring and evaluation of primary education. In it, characteristics common to many of the schools HM Inspectors have judged to be the most effective in recent years and procedures which schools might adopt to maintain and improve the quality of the service they provide, including the more systematic and consistent use of processes of self-evaluation, are identified. I hope that the report will be useful to all interested in primary education.

TN GALLACHER
HM Senior Chief Inspector of Schools

---

*Effective Secondary Schools, the first in the series, was published in 1988.

Introduction

Primary schools are responsible for a vital stage in education during which the foundations are laid for a lifetime of learning. The main purpose of this report is to provide primary schools with a basis for evaluating their own performance.

The report describes characteristics of good practice found in primary schools identified as effective by HM Inspectors of Schools during more than 600 inspections made over the last five years.

Although no school is likely to embody all the characteristics of effectiveness to the same extent, each should aim to improve its performance through a detailed consideration of the good practice contained in this report.

The report should be of interest to a wide audience, particularly teachers, school management teams, school boards, parents and education authorities.

CHAPTER ONE
Effective Learning and Teaching

To be effective primary education requires learning and teaching of high quality. This chapter, which is based on HM Inspectors' observations of effective practice, discusses what has to be learned; describes some of the characteristics of good learning and teaching; and considers ways of assessing whether or not the desired learning has taken place. Teachers are invited to evaluate their own practice in comparison with the features of effectiveness referred to in this chapter.

What has to be learned

1.1 A range of advice from national sources on the primary school curriculum has been available to schools in the form of HM Inspectorate reports and publications from the Scottish Consultative Council on the Curriculum (SCCC) and its committees on primary education. As a result, there is a measure of agreement nationally concerning the principles of good primary education. However, the evidence of inspection indicates that there is in practice an unacceptably high level of variation in the nature and quality of the planning and management of the curriculum across schools. In the most effective schools the curriculum is well planned and coordinated and provides pupils with a rich and rewarding experience; in others, however, the curriculum lacks sufficient breadth, is unbalanced or lacks coherence and progression for pupils. For that reason the Government has initiated a 5–14 Development Programme designed to lead to clearer definition of the content of the curriculum, the implementation of more systematic assessment policies and improved communication with parents about the nature and content of the curriculum and their children's progress through it. [*Curriculum and Assessment in Scotland: A Policy for the 90s* (SED, 1987)]

1.2 Interim guidance on the aims for primary education, the essential features of learning, the constituent elements of the curriculum and the balance of attention which should be given to them has already been provided in "*Curriculum and Assessment in Scotland: A policy for the 90s, Working Paper No 1: The Balance of the Primary Curriculum*", distributed to all teachers. Breadth and balance in the primary curriculum are expressed in terms of five broad areas: language, mathematics, environmental studies, expressive arts and religious and moral education. Detailed guidance in each of these areas is being formulated and will be issued in due course. This should enable all schools to emulate the good practice found in one primary school where:

> Teachers had a clear framework within which to plan their programmes and the headteacher, in discussing their forecasts with teachers, was able to promote development where this was required. Through her weekly visits to classrooms she was able to monitor class work and, in addition, she discussed their work informally with her staff at other times. As a result, a good balance was achieved in a broadly based curriculum and a sense of continuity and coherence was evident.

Effective practice

1.3 HM Inspectors find that effective learning takes place in classrooms where teachers:

i. establish and maintain a good classroom ethos in which pupils are motivated to learn;
ii. plan, prepare and organise lessons well and ensure that pupils are clear about what they have to learn;
iii. recognise the need for good classroom organisation including the organisation of resources;
iv. set a good example, and foster good relationships with pupils;
v. have high, but attainable, expectations of pupils in respect of both academic performance and good behaviour;
vi. provide tasks which are well matched to the needs, aptitudes and prior knowledge of individual pupils;
vii. understand the role of language in learning;
viii. ensure that pupils acquire knowledge, understanding and skills, are encouraged to become independent, resourceful and responsible, and are able to work purposefully on their own and with others;
ix. check that learning has taken place by ensuring that assessment is an integral part of classroom work and provides diagnostic information on pupil progress and information which can be used to evaluate their teaching and to inform parents; and
x. support classroom learning with work done at home where this is appropriate and in accordance with school policy.

The importance of ethos is discussed in the next chapter. The other key ideas noted above are now considered.

Planning

1.4 The evidence from inspections is that high standards of learning and teaching were found in those schools in which both long and short term curriculum planning were thorough. For example, in one school where:

> The school's educational policies are clearly set out in a series of detailed documents covering most areas of the curriculum. These papers identify the nature and scope of the curriculum and the school's preferred approaches to learning and teaching. Within this helpful framework class teachers prepare detailed forward plans of their work to an agreed format for the short and longer term. These plans also provide a useful framework for the school's developing procedures for assessment and record keeping.

1.5 Good curriculum planning involves careful consideration of breadth and balance. The five broad areas referred to in paragraph 1.2 provide a practical and convenient way of describing curriculum breadth but in reality the situation is much more complicated. These curricular areas merge or overlap in ways which make the definition of curriculum balance complex. In practice, curriculum balance cannot be defined rigidly in terms of a formula which applies in all situations. Each school must judge, within the limits of national and regional guidance, how best to achieve curriculum balance and there may be legitimate variations between schools. There may be variations in the balance among different stages in a school, at different times in the year and, to a limited extent, for pupils with particular needs or aptitudes. The curriculum should be balanced across the five broad areas so that each area is allocated the time and place necessary in order to achieve the aims set by the school. No area should be secured at the expense of another.

1.6 Teachers should also plan a balanced pattern for the pupils' day and week which ensures efficient use of time. For example, activities which require sustained concentration over an extended period of time should be balanced with activities of a less intense nature; and periods of quiet reflective study should be balanced by more active pursuits. Time will be required for direct teaching with the whole class, groups or individuals and for the assessment of pupils' progress. Considerations of balance may result in studies or subjects being allocated different lengths of time at different times of the day, week or year. For example, language and mathematics need not always be studied in the morning; environmental studies may have varying allocations of time from week to week. Attention should also be given to the balance of time pupils spend inside and outside school.

1.7 Careful consideration should be given to the continuity and coherence of the curriculum provided. Well-planned lessons take account of pupils' previous experiences, either within or outwith school, build on existing knowledge and understanding and respond flexibly to individual pupils' needs, aptitudes and interests. The capacity to make adjustments to plans depends upon continued monitoring of the activities undertaken by pupils and assessment of their progress. Plans should be sufficiently flexible to allow teachers to exploit learning opportunities afforded by unexpected current events of particular interest to pupils.

1.8 Teachers should plan and adopt approaches to learning and teaching which encourage active participation of pupils in the learning process such as, for example, open-ended enquiry, observing, investigating, experimenting and recording, and at the same time secure the development of appropriate knowledge, skills and understanding. These twin aims are most likely to be achieved through a judicious combination of subject based study and the well-planned study of topics or themes through which many effective teachers find that they can achieve a large number of their curricular aims. These latter approaches help pupils see the links between different curricular areas and between different kinds of knowledge; and can allow learning in one area to be reinforced and extended in others. However, within the study of such topics or themes, teachers must plan carefully to include a range of experiences which introduce pupils to required knowledge and understanding, allow the development and practice of specific skills, and promote appropriate attitudes.

1.9 The quality and extent of teachers' forward plans are of critical importance and it is essential that they should be considered and commented on by promoted staff, as in one school where:

> In addition to daily notes and plans, termly forecasts of work were drawn up by teachers and approved by the headteacher after discussion. The forecasts reflected school policy and referred to programmes of work for the different stages and for individual pupils.

Class organisation

1.10 Varieties of forms of class organisation are required if teachers are to meet the different needs of their pupils and provide all of them with appropriate work. In well organised classes pupils benefit from a judicious blend of whole class, group and individual learning and teaching. At times a small number of pupils will require the sustained support of the teacher while the rest of the class work purposefully on their own. At other times the pupils may be working individually or in groups on several different aspects of the curriculum while the teacher moves round the class asking challenging questions which probe understanding and help uncover learning difficulties. In one school teachers were highly skilled in class management:

> When group teaching took place the remainder of the class continued to work purposefully through a sequence of tasks explained by the teacher beforehand. The resources necessary to complete these assignments were clearly displayed in different parts of the classroom and pupils were trained to collect and return items as required. These orderly arrangements enabled pupils to work at their own level, particularly in language and, as the session progressed, in mathematics. At other times, depending on the nature of the lesson, all of the pupils in a class were taught together. Pupils responded well to these arrangements; they completed their schedules of work diligently and independently and, with sensitive support and direction, participated to the full in class and school activities.

1.11 Effective teachers vary the composition and size of groups in relation to the tasks being undertaken, having determined which learning experiences can be tackled by pupils in social groupings and which are best tackled by pupils of similar ability. Even in a small rural school with two teachers where there are normally two groups made up of pupils from P1–P3, and separately, P4–P7 there will be tasks which are best tackled by groups of pupils drawn from all stages of the school.

1.12 All teachers are accountable for the management of their own working areas. They should organise their classrooms efficiently, deploy their resources well and make them accessible to pupils. Classrooms should be safe, comfortable and stimulating environments for pupils. Relationships should be relaxed but purposeful and the overall atmosphere should promote the highest possible standards of work and behaviour.

Setting a good example

1.13 A distinguishing feature of effective teachers is their ability to create a climate of confidence and trust; to win the respect of their pupils. Because of their position of influence, all teachers should endeavour to set their pupils a good example in respect of, for instance, time-keeping, manner and appearance.

1.14 The quality of the relationship between the teacher and pupils is central to effective learning in any classroom. This is of particular importance in primary schools because a single teacher will normally be responsible for most if not all of the curricular experience of pupils in a class throughout a session. In carrying out this responsibility, most teachers are supported from time to time by other staff such as visiting specialists and learning support teachers as well as members of the promoted staff. Personal qualities associated with effective teaching include patience, understanding, fairness, drive, determination and a sense of humour. Teachers should have a calm but firm approach and a concern for their pupils' welfare, and a willingness to offer praise and reward when appropriate.

Teacher expectations

1.15 What pupils achieve depends to a significant extent on what their teachers think they are able to do. The case is well summarised in the following extract from an Inspectorate report:

> Such expectations relate to behaviour and attitude, and to the creation of a climate where pupils know, and generally accept, that only their best will do and that slipshod, careless work will not be acceptable. They come to expect from the businesslike atmosphere in which they find themselves that work given out will be called in, marked, commented on and returned quickly; and jotters, folders and notebooks will be checked for neatness and style. However, it goes beyond that to encompass an expectation of high achievement, which should not be confused with placing unrealistic demands upon the learner. On the other hand, targets should not be so low as to have the effect of reducing the levels of attainment which learners can achieve. Ascertaining the prior learning experience and individual strengths and weaknesses of pupils is important in order to differentiate expectations and teaching approaches. Research also shows that it is important to determine pupils' prior learning for another reason. If this knowledge is sound, further more complex ideas can be accommodated. Just as important, however, is the identification and rectification of half correct or even incorrect knowledge which otherwise hinders and sometimes totally prevents progress.

Matching tasks to individual pupils

1.16 Pupils differ in their needs, aptitudes and rates of progress depending on their background, previous experience, ability and motivation. Teachers have to take account of these differences by varying their expectations, their teaching approaches, the work they set for different pupils, and by ensuring that their concern extends to the whole ability range. In the most effective schools provision is made for pupils with learning difficulties and more able pupils as in the school where:

> The quality of teaching is good and a suitable range of class, group and individual activity is employed; groupings are organised to take account of age, aptitude and interest; . . . those pupils who have particular learning needs are well catered for, and she (the headteacher) demonstrates a close interest in the progress of all the pupils in the school. Teaching is designed to ensure that able pupils are suitably challenged.

1.17 It is most important that work in all areas of the curriculum should be matched to individual pupils' capabilities. Teachers are often most confident in dealing with the differing competences of pupils in reading and mathematics but it is much less common to find differentiated assignments or tasks in environmental studies or the expressive arts. However, failure to provide for the full range of abilities is not uncommon, even in reading and mathematics. In two schools inspected it was noted that:

> i. Teaching of reading at the early stages required some reappraisal. There was need to ensure that the differing abilities of the pupils were fully taken into account, that the various materials provided were carefully selected and that children were learning from them.
>
> ii. Throughout the school mathematics teaching was based on a published course supplemented by other texts . . . The work neither provided the opportunity to challenge the most able, nor did it ensure that the difficulties met by the least able were resolved.

The role of language

1.18 Good class teachers understand the fundamental role of language in learning. They give clear instructions when setting tasks so that what is to be learned, the key points of knowledge and understanding and the skills to be developed are presented logically and simply. Effective teachers create opportunities to talk with individual pupils, or with groups, as tasks proceed. They discuss the ideas involved, listen to pupils and encourage them to expand on points so that pupils are helped to develop their skills. Teachers should ask pupils challenging questions and extend understanding by suggesting alternative explanations or different lines of enquiry. Pupils should be encouraged to express themselves well and with confidence, as in one school where:

> Class discussions, for example, elicited imaginative and thoughtful responses from pupils. . . . Tape recordings were used to set contexts for drama and the children participated enthusiastically in the role-play involved. They were also able to recite poems which they had learned by heart. All were fluent speakers and most showed their command of a wide vocabulary and an ability to express themselves well.

Learning style

1.19 Inspection evidence suggests that pupils learn most effectively when they are actively involved in tasks which:

　i. provide first-hand experience involving, for example, manipulative skills, observation, measurement, data collection, analysis and interpretation;
　ii. require recording, reporting or an imaginative response using language or other forms of communication;
　iii. demand thought and allow the development and application of knowledge, understanding and skills in contexts or in solving problems;
　iv. involve the use of a range of interesting materials and a variety of learning strategies;
　v. require practice of the skills involved in finding out information; and

vi. give responsibility for ensuring that assignments are completed and for producing work of the best possible quality.

1.20 In schools where pupils were actively engaged in learning they were found to be approaching their studies "with excitement and enthusiasm" and "knowledgeable about what they had been studying". In one school, for example,

> Active learning was encouraged and the pupils at all stages had numerous opportunities to think, read and write for themselves, to talk with their teachers about what they were doing, to create their own pictures or craft objects and, in some classes, to learn from practical work and observation. Independence and confidence, along with co-operativeness, were characteristics of many pupils and all had the chance to contribute to group and class projects and to achieve some personal success in individual work.

In another school:

> The older pupils enjoyed many opportunities to learn not only through their own reading and research into books but also through discussion, observation, practical experience, visits, experiments and through thinking out, proposing and discussing solutions to various problems, often in the context of a family of imaginary characters.

Checking progress

1.21 Good learning and teaching are found where teachers see assessment as an integral part of their work, as in the school where:

> Assessment of pupils was mainly based on continuous appraisal of their work by teachers who used their observations to assist them in planning an appropriate teaching and learning programme. Pupils were responsible for keeping some of the records of their own performance in reading, spelling and mathematics.

1.22 Teachers use a range of assessment procedures to provide:

i. information which will enable the teacher, pupil, parents and other appropriate parties to judge the pupil's performance in each area of the curriculum;
ii. diagnostic information which will identify learning difficulties and inform the next phase in the pupil's learning;
iii. a view of the success of their teaching approaches and of the resources used;
iv. information which can be used in reviewing curriculum plans; and
v. pupils, parents, the school board and the education authority, as well as themselves, with evidence concerning the extent to which the school is achieving satisfactory standards of performance.

1.23 Pupils are more likely to make progress if they know how well they are performing. Teachers, parents and others concerned about the pupils' welfare also need to know so that they can take appropriate supportive action. Schools should take the initiative in establishing regular discussions with parents on pupils' performance and actively seek their interest and support in the next phase of the pupils' learning; headteachers should ensure that the diagnostic information yielded by assessment is put to good effect. Through discussion between teachers and the transfer of the evidence and results of assessments, continuity in teaching approaches is maintained as pupils move from one stage to another through the school. The following extract from one report illustrates what can be achieved:

> Pupil profiles were maintained by teachers with evaluative comments on pupils' performance in language arts, mathematics, environmental studies and expressive arts. Any learning difficulties being encountered by pupils and special interests of pupils were also noted and comments on attitude and behaviour were made. Profile entries were monitored by promoted staff and discussed with teachers. This form of information had proved useful for parent consultation evenings and accompanied the children as they progressed from stage to stage . . . Commendably pupils were encouraged to check their own work and completed a self-assessment diary.

1.24   HM Inspectors' reports make it clear that many schools need to give priority to developing effective assessment policies as an integral part of learning and teaching and to using the results of assessments when reviewing the curriculum. In addition, information on the attainment of pupils will be required for school boards. Section 10.3 of the *School Boards (Scotland) Act 1988* states that . . . "every headteacher shall provide to the School Board . . . an annual report including in particular a report on the level of attainment of the pupils in the school; . . ." Schools which do not have well-planned, efficiently implemented policies on assessment are failing to provide their pupils with opportunities and challenges to help them realise their full potential. Good management of these aspects within schools is a vital feature in determining the standard of education which they offer.

1.25   An important aspect of the 5–14 Development Programme will be the testing of each pupil in P4 and P7 in key aspects of English and mathematics on a nationally standardised basis. Also within the context of the 5–14 Development Programme, a committee on "Reporting" has been established to offer advice on issues relating to the reporting of pupils' progress and on the preparation and implementation of a new Pupils Progress Report (PPR).

Homework

1.26   Effective schools ask pupils to do work at home in line with an established school policy which takes account of the characteristics of pupils and the particular circumstances of the school. In one school, for example:

> There was a well thought out policy for homework which identified several purposes: to give additional practice in reading and spelling; to consolidate any work in which the child was experiencing difficulties; and to pursue local investigations outwith school time.

1.27   A number of schools have successfully broadened their approach to homework by including a range of imaginative exercises such as writing book reviews, commenting on particular television programmes, organising, conducting and reporting interviews, preparing for debates in school or drawing plans based on measurements made in and around the home. Homework provides a way of enabling parents to see examples of the kind of work being tackled during the school day and this is important in encouraging a sense of partnership between the school and parents.

CHAPTER TWO
Ethos and Partnership

Learning and teaching thrive best and pupils achieve high standards in schools with a good ethos. Pupils' progress and development are also influenced positively where schools and parents work in partnership. This chapter identifies a number of factors which contribute to the development of a good ethos and considers the importance of schools establishing supportive working relationships with parents, the wider community and other schools.

Ethos

2.1 An examination of HM Inspectors' reports shows that a good ethos in schools is associated with a range of factors which are highly supportive of learning and teaching and which help develop good social attitudes and behaviour in pupils. These factors include:

  i. high but attainable expectations of pupils' standards of work and behaviour;
 ii. teacher commitment and good morale:
iii. positive attitudes towards pupils and a concern for their well-being, coupled with a recognition of the motivating effect of praise;
 iv. strong and purposeful leadership by the headteacher, including a high level of support and encouragement for class teachers;
  v. a sense of identity and pride in the school;
 vi. recognition of the importance attached to appearances and to creating a welcoming environment;
vii. a concern to establish good relations with parents and the wider community;
viii. effective communication with parents and pupils; and
 ix. a willingness on the part of pupils and staff to be involved in extra-curricular activities.

The influence of teachers

2.2 Many of the above factors depend on the attitudes of class teachers and their view of the learning and teaching process. Teachers are major figures in the lives of their pupils and their behaviour is a powerful influence in shaping pupils' attitudes to learning and life. To promote the best classroom atmosphere, teachers have to be seen to be fair and firm in seeking and maintaining good standards of work and behaviour. Whatever teachers, or indeed schools expect of pupils in terms of attitudes and behaviour must be evident in the attitude and behaviour of teachers. Teachers were successful in promoting an atmosphere of courtesy and respect in one school where:

> The pupils were expected to develop high standards of personal conduct based on honesty and trust, and the success attained in this aim was evident in the amicable and mutually supportive atmosphere prevailing in the school. Relationships between staff and pupils were excellent; teachers were committed to the well-being and personal development of their pupils, both socially and educationally; pupils had good attitudes to learning and worked willingly and with a sense of enjoyment.

2.3   Teachers who are good listeners, and who give pupils opportunities to express their views, set an example for their pupils to follow when considering other people's opinions, values, culture and way of life as in the school where:

> Attitudes of care and responsibility towards others were fostered . . . The high value placed by teachers on the contributions of all pupils helped to establish excellent relations between children and adults.

It is not surprising that the report went on to commend the stimulating and encouraging climate in the school, adding that:

> Pupils responded well . . . participating enthusiastically in the life of the school, and displaying consideration and responsible behaviour at all times.

2.4   Good teachers promote pupils' self-esteem in a variety of ways including the recognition of worthwhile achievement. If teachers can increase their knowledge of pupils as individuals they are better able to offer them appropriate challenges. It is then more likely that pupils will have their self-regard enhanced by feelings of success and appreciation of their efforts. Self-discipline and self-control do not come easily to some pupils but because they are important factors in classroom harmony, and social relationships generally, they must be strongly encouraged.

2.5   A school with a good ethos shows evidence of concern for the general well-being of those who work in it. Procedures to ensure the welfare of pupils will be carefully considered and properly implemented by staff. These will include steps to monitor persistent late-coming and non-attendance and also the identification of any children showing signs of abuse.

2.6   Where a good ethos has been developed there will be an emphasis on the promotion and recognition of good behaviour. The expectations which teachers have of their pupils in terms of values, attitudes and behaviour are most likely to be realised if they are embodied in the life of the school. In one case, for example:

> The school's belief that children should grow to be mature and responsible individuals within a caring community was immediately illustrated for the visitor in the entrance foyer, where an attractive display combined useful information with exhibits of work and records of the achievements of past and present pupils. This approach set the tone in most classes where pupils were encouraged to take a pride in the school and in their work . . . They carried out assignments with enthusiasm and contributed willingly both to the life of the school and the wider community of the village it served.

Development of responsibility

2.7 A school with a good ethos tries to give all its pupils experience of responsibility and its expectations of them are well matched to their age and level of maturity. In one school, for example:

> The sense of purpose in the school derived not only from the guidance of the teachers but from the responsible way in which pupils followed through assigned tasks, individually or working together. From an early stage they showed that they could carry out tasks independently. For the older pupils it was accepted practice to choose their own place to work and the resources for their current task, and to work independently and effectively in different parts of the building. There was also a deliberate policy to give senior pupils responsibility for carrying out certain duties in the school.

2.8 Pupils benefit from being given responsibility for some organisational tasks which help the teacher manage classroom activities. Pupils working in a group and given responsibility for producing a mural or a short play learn how delegation and co-operation can affect the quality of the finished product. They should also be given some responsibility for their own learning and some choice in what they undertake. They should be encouraged to volunteer for the less attractive as well as the more obviously desirable tasks. Pupils should learn that the quality of the work they produce and its value to themselves and others depends to a large extent on the efforts they have made. In one school, for example, HM Inspectors noted that:

> The prevailing atmosphere in the school was harmonious, purposeful and orderly.
> . . . Capable class management and clearly defined expectations on the part of teachers helped the development of qualities such as tolerance and independence. Group activities, for example, were calculated to promote both autonomy and co-operation; . . . rosters for helping with classroom routines, distributing lesson materials and tidying up also fostered social skills and a sense of responsibility. Pupils were well motivated and displayed levels of maturity in their confidence, courtesy, and concern for others which often belied their years.

2.9 A sense of responsibility developed within the classroom extends to pupils' use of community facilities such as a public library or swimming pool. It is important for pupils to learn that self-control is compatible with enjoyment. There are many ways in which a school can give its pupils opportunities to behave responsibly. In one school, for example:

> An unusual and commendable feature of pupil responsibility was the election of pupil representatives to the staff-pupil council. Representatives came from P5 to P7 classes but each representative also took responsibility for reporting to and seeking the views of younger classes. The council discuss such issues as school sports, lunches, play facilities or starting a school magazine. Pupils took their responsibilities seriously and were not afraid to speak at meetings. There were instances of decisions having been taken and implemented to the benefit of all. This was good, practical training for participation in democracy.

Where a school promotes self-discipline, participation by pupils, co-operation and appropriate levels of competition, a stimulating school ethos is likely to result.

Partnerships with parents

2.10   Apart from its pupils, parents form the most important group of people with whom a school has to relate. The support and interest of parents can be of great value to a school. Recent research evidence confirms that parents do want to be involved in the life and work of the school attended by their children. The report, *"Home From School—Its Current Relevance"* (J. Macbeath, Jordanhill College of Education, 1988), highlights those aspects of school education which concern parents most and sets out what it is that parents expect of schools. Schools should compare their practice with the findings of the research so that they can evaluate the quality of their partnership with parents. The introduction of school boards will provide a further opportunity for parents to have a greater involvement in the education of their children. A school is more likely to have the support and trust of parents if it makes them welcome, offers them a range of contacts, sounds out their opinions and responds to their concerns.

2.11   An outward-looking school sees the statutory obligation to issue a handbook for parents as an opportunity to present itself, its aims, values and ideas in a positive way. Some schools have gone further and invited parents to give their views on the content and style of the handbook. The best of these go well beyond giving basic facts; they explain how the aims and policies of the school relate to classroom and other activities, and they give parents a clear idea of what is expected of them and what it is their children do in school. The point is summarised in one school report where:

> Careful arrangements were made to communicate with parents. The school handbook included a statement of aims and explained the organisation of the curriculum together with the school's teaching and assessment procedures. Advice about homework, information about the parents' association and administration details completed this comprehensive document.

Parents can also be informed of school activities by newsletters or school newspapers which pupils can play an important part in producing. Newsletters that are regular and helpful are much appreciated when they tell parents clearly what they want to know at the time they want to know it.

2.12   At the earliest stages of schooling parents are frequent visitors to classrooms as they bring and collect their children; this often allows good informal communication between teacher and parent. Sometimes parents are involved as helpers with play activities or in assisting with supervision on outside visits. The set occasions of parents' afternoons or evenings also allow useful contact to be made and maintained. Some schools have found it rewarding to establish weekly "activities afternoons" when parents come in to share their skills with pupils in such activities as music-making, photography, cookery or knitting. Many schools are helped by parents on sports days or in fund-raising fetes or galas. In one instance:

> Parents helped the school in a number of practical ways: assisting with the school bookshop, art and craft activities, school outings and organising resources. They also contributed spare materials for use in practical work and a number gave talks on hobbies and skills such as spinning or making Indian bread.

2.13   From the parents' point of view, the most important contacts with the school are by means of the regular written reports which they receive on their children's progress and attainments and the meetings they have with teachers soon afterwards. If parental support is to be enlisted in encouraging a child to change his or her behaviour, attitudes to work or attitudes to others, it is important that the reports communicate clearly and that their tone is appropriate. Parents are more likely to react positively to an adverse report, and feel that what staff have to say is well intended and worth taking seriously, if previous links with the school have been frequent, friendly and constructive.

Links with other schools

2.14   A successful school creates and maintains good links with other educational establishments. If there are nursery schools or playgroups in its area, good liaison and shared information help to smooth the passage of pupils into their first primary year. A common link with other primary schools is through sports activities which have an important role in promoting healthy attitudes towards participation, competition, winning and losing, fair play and acceptance of decisions made by others. Smaller or more remote schools can derive great benefit from co-operation with similarly placed schools to undertake joint ventures and visits which would otherwise be impractical or very expensive; the social contacts among pupils are not the least of the benefits.

2.15   All primary schools have some contact with the secondary schools to which their pupils transfer at the end of P7. Where good primary-secondary links exist, schools can trust each other's judgement, have a range of scheduled contact throughout the year to exchange information about pupils' progress and welfare, and co-operate in curricular matters to their mutual benefit. Increasingly, primary schools are being visited by secondary school pupils who are undertaking community service activities. It is important that these pupils should be made to feel welcome and useful.

2.16   Where primary and secondary links are at their best, the teachers at both stages have planned together continuity of learning, based on a shared understanding of the curriculum in their respective establishments, so that pupils experience a smoother transition between primary and secondary education. For example, in one school:

> The weekly visits of a member of the mathematics department to P6/7 to work with the class teacher and her reciprocal visits to his S1 class has forged close curricular links in that subject, . . .

Although the contacts between primary and secondary schools have improved over recent years, for example, with respect to the transfer of information about pupils and their needs, there is still considerable room for improvement, particularly in developing continuity of learning and teaching. *"Curriculum and Assessment in Scotland: A policy for the 90s"* recognises that "there is a serious problem of curricular discontinuity, especially in the four years between P6 and S2". The provision of a nationally agreed set of guidelines for each aspect of the curriculum for ages 5–14, setting out the aims of study, the content to be covered and the objectives to be achieved will help to tackle this problem and should be particularly helpful in promoting continuity and progression as pupils move from the primary to the secondary stage.

The wider community

2.17   Schools which have established good links in the community realise that local residents, businessmen and organisations have much to contribute to the preparation of young people for life beyond school. The treatment of visitors provides opportunities for social education; some pupils can be involved in the organisation of visits and in writing invitations and letters of thanks. Pupils learn to appreciate that certain visitors are volunteers, giving their time and knowledge freely, gaining no more than the satisfaction of having been of service. As well as the benefits of meeting visitors informally, pupils can gain insights into and awareness of the world of work when those such as fire and police officers are invited to the school. For example, in one case:

> The teachers had all established helpful networks of contacts in the wider community thus giving the children commendable awareness of local industry, shops and services through well prepared excursions from the school and through invitations to visitors to speak to classes.

2.18   It is important that a school is seen to be willing to devote time and energy to community concerns and welfare. The school may, for example, raise money for charity, clean-up a local amenity or undertake to enhance the environment by developing a nature trail. Each school should find its own way of making contributions which have value and significance for pupils and help develop ideals of responsibility and service as in the school where:

> Children and staff frequently undertook activities to help disadvantaged groups in the area, as when parcels of food were delivered to the elderly as part of the school's harvest festival theme.

The reputation of the school

2.19   A school which has successfully established a good ethos presents itself well to staff, pupils, parents and to the rest of the community. Visitors to the school gain a good impression if premises are free from litter and graffiti. This impression is enhanced by well-mounted displays of pupils' work in corridors and classrooms. Other displays of materials to interest and inform, such as photographs of school activities or well tended plants can be used to improve the attractiveness of social areas. In an effective school the visitor is unlikely to find teaching spaces that are silent but conversation and movement will be purposeful and orderly and pupils will be mindful of the need not to distract others who are concentrating on their own activities.

2.20   A school should wish to be well regarded by the community which it serves and should, therefore, make every effort to publicise its activities.

While the school handbook, mentioned earlier, is chiefly intended for parents, it should be made available to a wider audience and be attractive enough to warrant display, for example, in the local library. Occasional publications such as school magazines should be of as high a quality as possible in content and appearance, widely available, and sent with compliments to individuals and organisations who have been of service to the school. A local newspaper may be glad to hear of activities and initiatives or be willing to carry material produced by the school. The local library may welcome exhibitions of pupils' work and other exhibition areas should be explored for their potential. A school which has a proper self-confidence in its standards and its performance has everything to gain by spreading good news about itself.

CHAPTER THREE
Leadership and Management

The leadership qualities of headteachers and the manner in which they fulfil their management responsibilities are key factors in determining the effectiveness of their schools. While the detailed nature and pattern of management tasks may vary, depending on local circumstances, the basic principles of good management are common to all sizes and types of primary schools. In this chapter the characteristics which good leaders have in common are indicated and key aspects of management associated with effective learning and teaching are discussed.

Leadership

3.1 HM Inspectors' reports highlight the vital role of leadership in schools of all kinds. In one city centre school, for example, it was reported that:

> The efficiency of the organisation and management was a tribute to the calibre of leadership shown by the promoted staff and to the responsiveness and co-operation of the class teachers.

and in a small rural school it was noted that:

> Positive leadership has been provided by the headteacher through his roles as class teacher and manager. He leads by example and his supportive and respectful attitude to pupils, staff and parents . . .

3.2 In contrast, in one school where leadership with respect to aspects of curriculum development was weak it was noted that:

> Not all documentation issued was useful to the staff, nor had it all been fully discussed with them. Therefore, members of staff were unclear as to what was intended and some had difficulty in implementing the guidance in the classroom.

3.3 Leadership is about managing people so that they give of their best. Headteachers who are regarded as good leaders have a number of important characteristics in common. These include:

    i. having a strong commitment to the school, the parents and the community;

    ii. showing drive and determination and maintaining a high but purposeful profile in the school;

iii. creating appropriate expectations for teachers and pupils;
iv. showing concern for the welfare of staff and pupils;
v. setting a good example in professional terms;
vi. being open to personal approaches from pupils, parents and staff and listening to what they have to say;
vii. launching initiatives and taking responsibility for decisions;
viii. being able to motivate people and use praise and encouragement appropriately;
ix. being willing to consult others on significant issues; and
x. being honest, consistent and fair in dealing with others, thereby creating a climate of confidence and trust.

3.4 While no one will exhibit all of these characteristics to the same extent, none should be neglected and headteachers concerned to improve their leadership qualities would do well to examine their practice in the light of them.

Management responsibilities

3.5 Management responsibilities in primary schools occur in a variety of situations and levels. First, there are tasks for which the headteacher is directly responsible such as formulating policies and guidelines, monitoring and evaluating the work of the school, deploying staff, making best use of accommodation and resources, and liaising with other schools and external agencies. Secondly, there are responsibilities at classroom level which involve teachers in managing every aspect of their own work and that of their pupils for maximum effectiveness. These were considered in chapter 1. Thirdly, there are aspects for which all staff are responsible although the leadership offered by the headteacher will be a crucial factor, such as establishing a positive school ethos and maintaining a working partnership with parents; these were considered in chapter 2.

3.6 In large schools headteachers share their management duties with one or more promoted members of staff but in small schools the headteacher may have a full-time teaching commitment and indeed could even be the only permanent member of staff. Increasingly, education authorities are helping in these latter situations by providing assistance so that headteachers are freed from teaching commitments for part of the week to undertake management duties. In one school, for example:

> The headteacher, who takes the P5 class, uses the day a week when she is relieved of class teaching very effectively to attend to her management duties; she visits classrooms and provides support and advice to teachers. She has provided helpful guidelines for most aspects of the curriculum and has introduced a range of good learning and teaching materials; she has ensured that teachers prepare forward plans which she discusses with them; . . . and she consults teachers about priorities for development . . .

3.7 In areas with high levels of social difficulty a considerable amount of time may have to be devoted to dealing with problems arising directly from social circumstances. Often, difficulties manifest themselves in extreme behavioural problems. Work in such schools can be stressful and the headteacher should be concerned about the welfare of the staff. New members of staff may require training so that their expectations of pupils are appropriate and so that they employ methodologies suited to the special circumstances of the school.

Aims and policies

3.8 The best headteachers have aims which are clearly set out and understood by staff. These aims should meet the needs of pupils and take account of the views of parents. Headteachers should ensure that there are detailed policy papers on all major aspects of the school's work, indicating what is to be achieved and the approaches to be used.

3.9 Where a school has a sound base of good, well-documented policies, the benefits are substantial. Teachers have a clear idea of the structure in which they are to work and of the contribution they are to make; they see their teaching in the context of what everyone else is doing; and they have well-defined targets and guidance on how to attain them. Not least, pupils benefit as they move through the school; progress and development are smooth, building on what has gone before and preparing for what is yet to come. With changes of teacher there are no sudden changes of direction or styles of approach to bewilder or disconcert pupils. Headteachers should be prepared to support the implementation of policy as necessary. Good practice was observed where:

> The school was well and energetically managed. Class teachers were encouraged to take professional responsibility for the education of their pupils while working within the framework of whole school policies. The headteacher regularly spent a proportion of her time teaching with her colleagues, gaining a detailed knowledge of pupils and their work and joining directly in the variety of curriculum initiatives being taken in the school. She discussed with teachers their detailed forward plans and reviewed the format used in the light of staff comments. She had drawn up guidelines covering all the major areas of the primary curriculum and supplemented them by programmes of in-service training where it was felt that particular help was needed.

Policy development

3.10 The best school policies are produced through a process of staff consultation. They provide a detailed extension and interpretation of national and regional curriculum advice and give teachers a clearly defined framework for their own class planning. In effective schools the teachers operate as a team. Where staff have been fully consulted on matters affecting the whole school, they feel involved and are committed to the successful implementation of agreed policies. In one school which was "very well led", for example:

> She (the headteacher) has engaged staff in a continuing process of reviewing and defining school policies across a wide range of issues. Staff work well as a team and offer their individual talents to the benefit of each other's classes. Visiting specialists are drawn into this collaborative atmosphere and make very significant contributions to the overall work of the school.

In another school, however:

> A set of policy statements had been issued by the headteacher prior to the inspection but there had not been substantial consultation during their preparation nor briefing on their completion. As a consequence, teachers were not familiar with all of these documents and their own plans for art, music, physical education, environmental studies and, in some respects, language skills lacked the clarity and consistency which a well understood policy for the curriculum of the school as a whole could have brought about.

3.11   In the process of policy-making, consultation should not always be confined to the teaching staff. There are occasions when parents should be consulted, for example, on health education or out-of-school visits. In future the school board will be an important forum for consultation and the exchange of information.

3.12   The whole-staff meeting is the simplest means of internal consultation. In larger schools there can be stage meetings and internal working parties. Whatever the purpose of such meetings, they require to be carefully planned and followed up if they are to be worthwhile. There should be a clear agenda or programme, published well enough in advance to allow for adequate thinking and preparation. Minutes should be kept of meetings and the decisions taken confirmed to all concerned. The successful chairing of such meetings calls for a range of skills, not the least of which is securing the participation of every member of the group. The maintenance of a general atmosphere of trust and respect for each other's views is clearly important. In one school, for example:

> Since 1984, weekly staff meetings have provided a forum for discussion of new ideas and materials and for reports from teachers who have attended in-service training courses; . . . the learning support teacher has contributed regularly to these discussions.

3.13   Teachers in small schools have a particular need to discuss policy with others on a regular basis. Some education authorities bring the headteachers of their small schools together to share experience and difficulties and to exchange information on procedures which have proved useful in their particular circumstances. There is, however, much that individual headteachers can do to help themselves. In one small school, for example:

> The headteacher has made determined efforts to overcome her isolated position and keep up-to-date with developments in primary education . . . she has maintained regular telephone contact with the primary adviser, and requested and received support in the form of advice and, at times, resources. She has also tried to maintain personal contact with the headteachers of the nearest similar small schools and makes good use of the facilities of the Divisional resource library and the public library service.

3.14   Schools must change as society and its expectations change, and other changes result from planned improvements in teaching methods or curriculum and assessment arrangements. For example, there is current discussion about the introduction of modern languages into the primary curriculum. Other changes result from advances in technology: the most obvious example is the general availability of relatively inexpensive electronic equipment such as the calculator and the microcomputer with its ever increasing range of programs. Schools have to be able to adjust their policies and guidelines in response to such innovations. Increasingly good use is being made of microcomputers, as in the school in which:

> The microcomputer is used regularly at all stages to reinforce skills, explore understanding of concepts and occasionally to create problem-solving situations . . .

The role of other promoted staff

3.15 Promoted staff, whether assistant or depute headteachers, should have clearly defined remits agreed with the headteacher. Good headteachers deploy the staff allocated to their schools so that promoted staff have enough management time available to fulfil their remits. If promoted staff are to work effectively as a team, it is important that they meet to discuss and plan the work of the school regularly. Good team work was evident in one school where:

> The headteacher, the depute and the assistant headteacher worked well as a management team; each member had a clear remit. There were well-defined arrangements for the management of different stages, budgeting and selection of resources, the induction of new teachers and liaison with parents. The team met frequently to review the curriculum, organise staff development and make the administrative arrangements necessary for the smooth running of the school. A formal minute of its meetings recorded the matters considered; there was invariably a follow-up discussion at a subsequent meeting of all staff. Some issues were taken further at the weekly planned activity time or during the days set aside for in-service training . . . In many instances they led by example by demonstrating new approaches either within their own classes or by working alongside other teachers.

3.16 The remits of depute and assistant headteachers vary from school to school but they tend to cover most, if not all, of the following responsibilities:

i. developing and monitoring policies in a curriculum area or at a particular stage of the school;
ii. ensuring effective forward planning, record-keeping and class management by individual class teachers;
iii. providing a positive lead in the practice of teaching by demonstrating techniques to colleagues within co-operative and team teaching arrangements;
iv. piloting innovatory work;
v. providing particular support to groups of pupils such as children with special aptitudes or pupils with learning difficulties;
vi. contributing to various classes in particular curriculum areas where staff expertise may be lacking;
vii. planning and supervising the use of resources in the school;
viii. deploying staff to make the most effective use of their capabilities;
ix. providing appropriate advice and support to teachers including probationers and non-teaching staff; and
x. promoting effective links with parents and the wider community.

In one school, for example:

> Both assistant headteachers had balanced remits covering the supervision of learning and teaching of certain classes, curriculum development throughout the school and administration. One was responsible for the supervision of P1–P3, for reading and music at all stages and for the organisation of the annual visit by P7 to London. She gave a substantial part of her time each week to helping individuals and small groups of children in P1–P5 with reading. The other was responsible for the supervision of P4–P7, for mathematics throughout the school, arrangements for the use of accommodation, broadcasts, visits to the locality and the recreational programme for P4–P7. She also worked with groups of children from most stages of the school, in class and by withdrawal, to give help with learning difficulties and to develop the interests of children with special aptitudes.

3.17 Promoted staff are often given responsibility for particular stages of the school. The development of post-graduate qualifications has equipped many depute and assistant headteachers with additional skills and knowledge which have helped to make the organisation of work at particular stages more effective. The balance in the expertise of the management team should be kept in mind by those responsible for appointing replacement promoted staff.

Monitoring performance

3.18 It is not enough for a headteacher to produce policy statements and guidelines. Their implementation must be systematically monitored. In too many schools it was found that policy statements "were neither being implemented in classrooms nor being monitored by promoted staff. As guidelines they were incomplete and too general to give practical help to teachers . . ."

3.19 The best classroom teaching is normally based on careful forward planning. Regular discussion of teachers' forward plans allows promoted staff to identify where and when teachers need support and to monitor the implementation of school policies. This was evident in one school where:

> The quality of the curriculum for all pupils was monitored carefully by promoted staff and class teachers. All teachers planned their work for a month ahead and submitted these and the details of weekly work to the promoted staff. Class teachers were also able to adjust their programme as they evaluated the degree to which all pupils were managing various aspects of the work.

The approach to forward planning, however, varies between schools and may even lack consistency within a school as in one case where it was noted that:

> Teachers regularly submitted plans of the work which they intended to undertake but the format used for such submissions varied from teacher to teacher. There would be benefit in establishing a common structure for these plans which could then be used as a basis for discussion about balance and progression in the curriculum.

3.20 While monitoring is primarily a responsibility of headteachers, in larger schools it is reasonable for them to delegate part of this function to other promoted staff. Whoever undertakes this task, it is important that teachers see it as a constructive and supportive activity, in which they are contributing to the systematic evaluation and development of the school's policies and practices.

Administration

3.21 Headteachers are responsible for ensuring that the school is administered efficiently. Administrative duties fall into two broad categories. First, the headteacher has to provide information which is required by the education authority and the Scottish Education Department on such matters as attendance and staffing. Secondly, they have to ensure that appropriate arrangements are made for all aspects involved in the day-to-day running of the school such as coping with staff absences, organising school functions and external visits, ordering and taking delivery of materials, typing and reprographics, transport arrangements, maintaining records, responding to external contacts and dealing with emergencies. Where possible, these tasks should be delegated to assistant headteachers, teachers or in certain cases, to non-teaching staff.

Management of resources

3.22 A school should have a policy for the acquisition, distribution and use of teaching materials and equipment. An efficient school will maintain an up-to-date record of teaching materials and will have clearly understood and practised procedures for gaining access to them and a system for ensuring their maintenance and replacement as necessary. Timetabling the use of certain resources is also important. It can, for example, help to ensure that teachers incorporate the microcomputer, radio, VCR, or TV in their teaching and take full advantage of the school's equipment for physical education or music. In one school for example:

> Much thought had been given to the organisation and storage of materials. There was systematic and planned use of microcomputers. Arrangements for taking radio and television broadcasts were carefully timetabled. Very effective use had been made of the resources offered by the local area and its community . . .

Where parents and staff have played a considerable part in contributing to or raising funds for resources, they should play a part in deciding how the funds are spent.

Management of accommodation

3.23 Learning and teaching will be adversely affected if accommodation is not used in an appropriate way. For example it was noted in one school that:

> The accommodation available was not being used to full advantage. From P3 to P7 the activity areas, the general purpose rooms and the spare classroom were under-used, for example. The use of the assembly hall stage as a television viewing area was unsatisfactory because of the noise generated by classes taking physical education. Conversely, pupils in the gymnasium sometimes had difficulty in hearing teachers' instructions clearly.

3.24 Decisions about the use of available space should be governed by the school's policy for learning and teaching. As rolls change it is important to consider alternative uses of accommodation; any decisions should be based on consultation with staff. Although variation in the use of rooms may be more difficult in older schools, there is frequently potential for more flexible use of space. Modern buildings are often designed with flexible use in mind.

Staff deployment

3.25 When deploying staff a headteacher has to take account of the needs of particular classes, the particular aptitudes and experience of teachers, their preferences and the need to extend their experience. Teachers who have particular skills, for example, in science, music, drama or art, may sometimes be deployed with classes other than their own. Where for any reason a class has more than one teacher for a substantial part of the week, care is needed to ensure continuity in the curriculum.

3.26 The provision of learning support specialists varies from one authority to another and where they are available to provide help and support for children with learning difficulties they are deployed in a number of different ways. Effective practice was observed in one school where:

> Standardised tests of reading and number administered at the P2 and P3 stages respectively help to identify those pupils who require support with their learning. Both those pupils with learning difficulties and the ablest receive first-rate support from the visiting remedial teacher. She occasionally withdraws pupils to tackle specific difficulties, but mostly works in classrooms alongside teachers helping pupils in whatever aspects of the curriculum they need support. Good diagnostic assessment and record keeping contribute to the effectiveness of the well-judged learning support.

3.27 Visiting teachers and specialists should be carefully deployed to benefit the maximum number of pupils and staff. Where the number of classes directly involved is limited, arrangements should be made to allow specialists to operate as consultants to the others on a regular basis and as part of any in-service training. It is important to regard visiting teachers as an integral part of the whole staff team. They should be aware of the school's aims, policies and guidelines and be encouraged to contribute to their development.

3.28 Staff appointed to the recently created posts of senior teachers should have significant responsibilities. The new post holders should be given the opportunity to share their expertise with colleagues. Given their role as illustrators of good classroom practice, it is important that other staff are in a position to learn from their example.

Staff development

3.29 In order to realise the full professional potential of each member of staff and meet the needs of the school, headteachers must ensure that teachers have regular opportunities for professional growth and development. One of the most effective approaches to professional development is to enable staff to teach alongside colleagues in their own classrooms. In-service training courses offered by various agencies should be carefully considered to see whether they meet the needs of the school or individual staff development programmes. Sometimes college of education staff, advisers or staff tutors, may be invited to work directly with staff in schools. Visits to other schools can also introduce new perspectives. More frequently, promoted staff will call on expertise within the school and organise internal opportunities for staff development through staff and stage meetings, classroom visits and individual consultations. Work such as this requires a good awareness by management of what staff have to offer and also a knowledge of the available range of advice, literature and training resources such as videos, broadcasts and distance learning packages. Participation in school-based training both as a learner and contributor is an important part of a teacher's professional development. An example of good practice was found in one school where:

> As part of a staff development programme, the promoted staff were closely involved in providing practical assistance to teachers in the classrooms and in advising upon their forward programmes of work. The staff complement included a significant number of new or inexperienced class teachers. In-service training days had, therefore, assumed critical importance in the school calendar, and senior staff and more experienced teachers had played a role in leading group meetings to discuss and advise upon problems. The value of this work was additionally important to the school in view of the significant social and educational problems with which it had to deal.

3.30 Teachers' conditions of service allow for significant amounts of time to be made available each year for teachers to undertake in-service training. In many schools planned activity time and in-service days have been used purposefully to share expertise and experience, as in one school where, for example:

> All teachers participated in a varied programme of staff training, devised by the headteacher, using time available under the terms of the teachers' conditions of service. A feature of the programme was the full use of staff expertise, the education authority advisory service, visiting teachers and secondary school staff.

When drawing up a training programme, special attention should be given to the needs of particular members of staff. For example, probationer teachers should be supported with a clearly defined programme of induction which should include regular interviews with promoted staff and opportunities for the promoted staff to observe classroom practice. At the same time the overall programme should be monitored to ensure an appropriate breadth of training.

3.31 Management training for headteachers will receive a major stimulus as a result of the Scottish Education Department's initiative involving the preparation of eight training modules covering the key aspects of the management of schools. The main objective is to enhance the expertise of serving headteachers, with many of their development needs and those of other promoted staff being met by education authority courses based on the nationally developed management training modules, by using associated open learning materials and joint activities with colleagues from other schools.

3.32 Headteachers should be caring of staff welfare and the need to create the right atmosphere in the school; quick to express informed appreciation of good work and commitment; sensitive to any stressful circumstances affecting their staff; and able to offer support and advice without becoming obtrusive. Where necessary, they must be constructively critical, firm in their insistence that staff adhere to agreed school policies and in extreme cases willing and able to invoke disciplinary procedures.

Non-teaching staff

3.33 The headteacher should ensure that *all* staff are aware of the aims of the school and that they *all* co-operate in seeking to achieve them. Clear guidelines should be given regarding the remits of non-teaching staff. The school secretary, janitors, cleaners, kitchen staff, clerical assistants and auxiliaries have a vital role to play in the smooth running of the school and in maintaining the quality of the school's environment. Those who meet visitors to the school have an important responsibility for the creation and maintenance of good impressions. Auxiliaries have a key role as they are deployed over a wide range of duties involving contact with both staff and pupils. Their duties can include maintaining the school's resources, distributing materials, supervisory activities directed by teaching staff and some clerical work.

Evaluating practice

3.34 Finally, ensuring that practice in classrooms is adequately monitored and that key aspects of the work of the school are subject to systematic evaluation are among the most important aspects of the work of the headteacher. Although it can be argued that all teachers have a duty to evaluate their own performance, the principal responsibility for ensuring that this happens lies with the headteacher. If the best conditions for sound learning and teaching are to be created and maintained in a school, then the formulation and implementation of a considered policy for systematic self-evaluation must be given high priority.

CHAPTER FOUR

Accountability and Evaluation

Schools are accountable for the quality of the education they provide and the levels of attainment achieved by the pupils entrusted to them. The aim of this chapter is to encourage schools to undertake self-evaluation and suggest possible ways forward.

Accountability

4.1   Apart from pupils, parents are a school's most important client group. The national initiative which gave parents choice of school ("The Parents' Charter") extended local accountability and brought about an increased awareness in schools of the need to present themselves positively to parents and the wider community.

4.2   The handbook which is issued to parents by each school annually deals with important issues such as the school's educational aims, the breadth and balance of the curriculum at different stages, the arrangements for assessing and reporting pupils' progress, the ways in which the school seeks to consult and involve parents, and the organisational procedures needed to make the school a safe, pleasant and well-organised environment for pupils. Many schools offer parents an insight into their work through a range of activities to which parents are invited and some have more formal arrangements involving parent-teacher associations.

4.3   The introduction of elected school boards, with a majority of parent members, will extend accountability still further and give it a new local form. The school board will have a range of responsibilities and the right to be informed about any aspect of the school's policies and practices. In order to respond to the increasing emphasis on accountability schools will have to develop more systematic and effective approaches to self-evaluation and to the presentation of information about their organisation and performance.

4.4   On-going internal evaluation is not only important as a basis for rendering an account to parents, it is an integral and important part of the management process. Every school should have educational aims which are appropriate to its pupils and community, and in a good school these aims should be kept under review by the headteacher in consultation with interested parties such as school staff, parents, the school board and the education authority. Once aims are set, the level of a school's performance can be determined by the extent to which the agreed aims are achieved through the implementation of the school's policies. A planned approach to evaluation will establish those aspects of policy or implementation which are satisfactory and those which require further development. Poor or non-existent evaluation procedures are incompatible with effective management.

External and internal evaluation

4.5 An effective system of school evaluation will contain elements of both external and internal evaluation. External evaluation has the advantages that: it can provide an independent check of the school's performance in relation to generally accepted regional or national standards; it can afford insights not always evident to those closely involved in the work of the school; and it can offer a wider perspective in terms of possible developments in policy and practice. A good example of external school evaluation is the programme of inspections regularly carried out by HM Inspectors.

4.6 Internal evaluation has many advantages: it need not disrupt normal patterns of working; it can be more or less continuous and be extended to any aspect of the school's work; it lays emphasis on teachers' professionalism and appears less threatening than external evaluation. It should be well informed as it is undertaken by those who know most about the situation being evaluated and it should be effective since its results are immediately available to those best placed to act upon them.

4.7 Self-evaluation takes place when staff, working individually or in groups, monitor and judge the effectiveness of the school's work. Whenever teachers consider more effective layouts for their classrooms, or a school considers the need to change a reading scheme or a mathematics programme, the existing provision is being examined with a view to its improvement and that is the essence of self-evaluation. There is now an increasing awareness that schools should develop a more systematic and effective approach to this aspect of their work. Initially, the term self-evaluation may strike some teachers as forbidding but their reservations should disappear as they realise that its purpose is to make their schools more effective and their jobs more satisfying.

4.8 Internal evaluation should be a continuous process in which each member of staff plays an important part. This is not to suggest that schools should be in a non-stop ferment of self-examination and self-questioning but that each school has a responsibility to develop in response to changes in society, the needs of the community, the concerns of parents, the findings of research in education, and the availability of new and improved resources. No school can afford to become complacent or static. A successful headteacher does not see change as an end in itself but as a means of improving performance, enhancing achievement and raising standards.

Starting points for self-evaluation

4.9 An initiative may be undertaken by a school in response to an HM Inspector's report, to proposals made by the education authority or as part of its own management policy and practice. In future the impetus could come from the deliberations of the school board.

4.10 A number of education authorities have offered advice on school evaluation or are in the process of doing so. In one case a system has been established whereby schools undertake evaluation using a common approach and make an annual report to the authority. Some education authorities have distributed papers analysing the main issues commonly identified in HM Inspectors' reports and asked schools to evaluate their performance with reference to them. These initiatives should lead to steady improvements in the quality of provision in the areas concerned and point the way forward for others.

Preparation

4.11 Whatever the stimulus, experience indicates that effective self-evaluation takes place only when care has been taken to create the right conditions. A proper climate can be established by:

   i. ensuring staff are clear about the purposes and value of the exercise;
   ii. promoting staff discussion of issues associated with school effectiveness;
   iii. consulting staff at all levels in advance so that they can help plan the procedures to be used; and
   iv. ensuring that the programme is realistic and practicable and that all staff understand their part in it.

4.12 If the school's links with parents are to be reviewed, a necessary condition for success is the establishment of a good working partnership. If pupils are to be consulted, as may well be appropriate, then the necessary groundwork must be done in that area too. Although the establishment of the right climate for evaluation may well be difficult, the process of being consulted, having one's opinions seriously considered, feeling that one's contributions are valued and that they may result in change for the better are all powerful builders of morale, confidence and commitment.

The way forward

4.13 The first step is to establish agreed criteria for satisfactory performance in a range of aspects covering the quality of learning and teaching, pupil and parent satisfaction, ethos and management. The criteria should be produced through a process of consultation and be clearly stated in school documents. In establishing the criteria headteachers will draw on their own and their staff's experience and make use of guidance offered by their education authority and the Scottish Education Department. This report is also a useful source of advice since each chapter outlines key features of effectiveness based on good practice seen in many schools which can be used to establish performance criteria. The second step is to determine current levels of performance so that those aspects of the school's work in need of development can be identified. Most schools will identify a number of aspects and headteachers should establish priorities to ensure that the response is focused and practicable.

4.14 Current levels of performance can be determined by:

i. monitoring by teachers of particular aspects of learning and teaching in their own classrooms (sometimes they are assisted in this by a colleague or a member of the promoted staff);
ii. analyses of selected pupil work and the results of pupil assessment, and monitoring of standards of pupil attainment;
iii. discussion between promoted staff and individual teachers on the teachers' forward plans;
iv. discussion by staff of school policies and their implementation;
v. monitoring of aspects of the school such as pupil behaviour, attendance and the incidence of particular types of learning difficulties; and
vi. canvassing of the views of pupils, parents and other interested parties.

4.15 Experience shows that checklists and questionnaires can often be used to good effect. The formulation of such instruments can be a valuable exercise in itself but it is time-consuming and demands considerable skill. Wherever possible, schools should make use of evaluation materials already developed by education authorities and other agencies. Although the details of the approaches used by individual schools to evaluate their own practices depend on their particular circumstances, there are some common features. For example, most schools where internal evaluation has been carried out successfully:

i. ensure that a manageable quantity of relevant evidence is collected at the outset;
ii. use or adapt techniques already developed and tested elsewhere, thereby saving time;
iii. ensure that the self-evaluation exercise allows staff to draw conclusions which can give rise to action; and
iv. build in a system for on-going review and evaluation of the implementation of any agreed policies.

Conclusion

4.16 A school should have effective procedures for evaluating its performance on a continuing basis. In the best primary schools, evaluation is already an integral part of the everyday activity of headteachers and classroom teachers. The expectation is that all schools can learn from the best practice already in evidence. Maximum effectiveness must be the ideal which informs and motivates the life and work of a school.